The Pride, Fall and Restitution of King Nebuchadnezzar

By Henry Smith

The Pride, Fall and Restitution of King Nebuchadnezzar
By Henry Smith

Edited and updated by C. Matthew McMahon and Therese B. McMahon
Transcribed by Beth Saathoff

Published by Puritan Publications
A Ministry of A Puritan's Mind
4101 Coral Tree Circle #214
Coconut Creek, FL 33073
www.puritanshop.com
www.apuritansmind.com
www.puritanpublications.com

This Print Edition, 2013
Electronic Edition, 2013
Manufactured in the United States of America

ISBN: 978-1-62663-011-6
eISBN: 978-1-62663-010-9

Front cover by William Blake (1757-1827), called "Nebuchadnezzar" painted in 1795.

TABLE OF CONTENTS

MEET HENRY SMITH

Henry Smith, who is apostrophized in Piers *Penniless' Supplication* (1592) as *Silver-tongued Smith*, was a celebrated preacher in Elizabethan London at St. Clement Danes. On leaving Queens' College, Cambridge, he continued his studies with Richard Greenham, rector of Dry Drayton, Cambridgeshire, who imbued him with Puritan principles as he did other leading men of the time. In 1575 he also entered Lincoln College, Oxford, graduating in 1579.

Though, as the eldest son and heir of Erasmus Smith of Somerby and Husbands Bosworth, Leicestershire, he was heir-apparent to a large patrimony, he prepared to enter the Ministry of the

Church, but, owing to conscientious scruples on the matter of subscription, he determined not to undertake a pastoral charge, but to content himself with a Lectureship. Strype, in his Life of Bishop Aylmer, speaks of Smith as "an eloquent and witty man who in 1587 became Reader or Lecturer at St. Clement Danes, at the desire of many of the parishioners, and by the favor of the Lord Treasurer who dwelt in the same parish and yielded contribution to him."

Thomas Fuller also, in *A Life of Henry Smith* which he prefixed to the first *Collected Edition* of his works, said of him: "He was commonly called the Silver-tongued preacher, and that was but one metal below St. Chrysostom himself. His Church was so crowded with auditors that persons of good quality brought their own pews with them, I mean their legs, to stand thereon in the alleys. Their ears did so attend to his lips, their hearts to their ears, that he held the rudder of their affections in his hands, so that he could steer them whither he was pleased."

Wood, too, tells us that Smith was "esteemed the miracle and wonder of his age, for his prodigious memory and for his fluent, eloquent and practical way of preaching." (*Athenae Oxon.* i. p. 603). And in our own time Marsden, in his *History of the Puritans*, has described Smith's Sermons as "noble examples of English prose and pulpit eloquence, and as being free in an astonishing degree from the besetting vices of his age—vulgarity and quaintness and affected learning."

Owing to ill-health he resigned his Lectureship about the end of 1590, and retired to Husbands Bosworth, where he died the following summer, and was buried July 4th, 1591, although some (like Brooks) place his death at 1600.

His *Collected Sermons* passed through the following editions:—1592, 1593, 1594, 1595, 1599, 1604, 1607, 1609, 1612, 1613, 1614, 1617, 1618, 1619, 1620, 1621, 1622, 1631 and 1632. Also added is Puritan Publications' first collection of his sermons in the work, "The Calling, Rebellion and Punishment of

Jonah, and Other Sermons," which is a fantastic treatment of the book of Jonah. This current volume is specially designated to deal with lessons gleaned from the life of King Nebuchadnezzar, demonstrating how his pride opened the door to his fall, and then final restitution by God's grace. Smith's sermons in this work are outstanding, and though they are primarily relevant to kings, presidents and those in such authoritative position, they are equally relevant to Christians who must deal with the sins of pride and vainglory each day they live in this world regardless of their station in life.

J.B. and C.M.M.

March 1, 2013

PART 1: THE PRIDE OF KING NEBUCHADNEZZAR

"At the end of twelve months he walked in the palace of the kingdom of Babylon. And the king spake, and said, Is not this great Babylon, that I have built for the house of the kingdom by the might of my power, and for the honor of my majesty?" (Daniel 4:29-30).

I have chosen this story of Nebuchadnezzar so that you may see his pride, his fall, and his restitution. This Nebuchadnezzar was a wicked king; and therefore, God warned him by a dream and by Daniel to amend his life, but he would not serve God. He made many shows, but revolted again; therefore, at the last, God gave him over for a time, and he became like a beast until he acknowledged that his power comes from God. A warning to all rulers to remember that one Ruler is above which they all must serve, or else all their buildings, treasures, and guard will not shield them from judgment when the stroke comes, no more than they could save Nebuchadnezzar.

At the end of twelve months—says Daniel—this king willed evil in his royal palaces. The prophet shows that he had deserved this punishment before, and that his dream which he had told him, that his kingdom should depart from him for his pride; yet this respite was granted to him for twelve months—like the forty days which were granted to the Ninevites, (Jonah 3:4-5)—to try what he would do upon his warning, and whether he would repent as the Ninevites did. Therefore, the Holy Spirit shows how the time ran and how he lived after. This is as if he should say, *if he would return yet and be warned by the dreams and by the prophet which I sent him, I will stay my hand, and his kingdom shall not depart from him.* But here he shows that he forgot his dream—like a dream—and was more desirous to know what it meant than to be warned by it (the twelve months ran month after month). Now his dreams are gone, and he thinks that all has ended; yet Nebuchadnezzar is all alone. Therefore, he goes to his palace amidst his delights to bake himself, as it were, in the sun of all his pleasures, where indeed he hastened God to take all his pleasures from him when he should have repented—as Daniel willed him—ripped up his sins, bewailed his life, poured forth tears, and prevented his judgment with prayer on his knees. Then he was walking in his galleries and thinking what sin should be next, to fill up the number of his rebellions, that God might not spare him when he judged him.

The wicked will not suffer the prophecies of God against them to be vain, but they will set before God, in mind of their punishment, and sin until the punishment comes to fulfill the threatening due to them.

Some think that Nebuchadnezzar walked on the roof of his palace from where he might see all parts of the city round about him. Like the mountain where the tempter led Christ, to show him the beauty of the world, (Matt. 4:8).

Daniel would signify that the king lived in ease as he lived before and pleased himself still in vanity, for all his warning, and turned his time of repentance to sin. Therefore, the Lord would defer no longer, but cut him down like the barren fig tree, (Matt. 3:10). He did this to teach us to take mercy while it is offered, to repent while we have time, and if God speaks but once to us, to lay it up in our hearts forever, not look to be spoken to again, because God is not bound to warn us at all. One would have thought that Nebuchadnezzar would have remembered his warning while he lived because he had such a strange and fearful dream, then another dream to confirm it, and then a prophet to expound it with the exposition of it threatening such a downfall to himself. One would have thought he could not have forgotten it though he had lived until this day. But like a wonder, which lasts but nine days, so is the repentance of them that are accustomed to sin. When sin is rooted, it sticks hard, and who shall weed it? Though God should send us dreams, though he should show us a vision, though he should raise up prophets, Daniel himself cannot make this *Black Moor* white which has always been black. We may see this in ourselves, for that we need is to hear of repentance often, more than of anything else, but it is such a thing what we cannot *conceive* to do. If we are warned of anything but of sin, one warning will serve, but we are so incorporated and inured with sin, that a thousand sermons will not serve; so custom has made sin stronger in many than the word of God. We remember, or consider, or apply it how we will, after twelve months God will come and take account of his dreams and of his prophet which he sent to see what Nebuchadnezzar has profited by them. Although he has leaden feet, which are long a coming, yet he has iron hands, which when he comes will strike home.

Now God comes and finds Nebuchadnezzar on his towers, when he should have cast himself down to the ground and thought on his dreams and Daniel, to humble his pride. He was perched on his roof, and there he begins to *crow* of his wealth: *Is not this great Babylon, that I have built for the house of the kingdom by the might of my power, and for the honor of my majesty?* See how the man stands in admiration of his vanity. He is like a usurer which dotes on his money as though he had deserved immortal fame for spending his money vainly, to lay one stone on another.

*Is not this great Babylon...*he *should* have said: *Is not this Nebuchadnezzar's folly*, which he has built to mock his name and to impeach his wisdom, for men to say when they pass by: *Look how our king has bestowed his revenues; here lie our subsidies and our tributes in these stone walls?* But Nebuchadnezzar thinks that every man will praise him for his folly. Therefore, as a woman who is urged on in her splendor, thinks that all admire her and have a good opinion of her—as the peacock has of his feathers—and she frames all of her tricks, speeches, and gestures accordingly. So when Nebuchadnezzar sat in his palace and saw such fine things about him, his pride says: *You must frame your looks, gestures, and speeches accordingly, or else your palace will be more splendid than the king himself.* So he begins to exalt his mind higher than his palace and to look and speak out more than he did before. The temptation was no sooner in his heart, than it was in his mouth, and he pleased himself therein so well that he could not refrain, being alone, just as a fool admires himself in a glass, so he, with nobody with him, strutted alone and bragged by himself, to think what a jolly fellow he was. Now men begin to talk of his buildings. By this we may see how wealth and honor change manners and how a nice coat, or a worked handkerchief, or a gold ring can make a man's mind *showy* and make him look and speak after another fashion than he previously did. It is a wonder to see what power these petty, vain toys have over the mind, to alter and change a man suddenly when he thinks better of himself that day he wears them than any other day.

*Is not this great Babylon...*before the Holy Spirit abates Nebuchadnezzar's words, mark how he comes to them. *The king spoke and said:* Was one not enough, but he must say, *speak and said?* This doubling of the words shows that he spoke with a premeditated pride from the root of his heart, which should reveal whether or not it was sin, come what may. For the Holy Spirit brings in other speeches with *"he said"* and no more. But here he says, *"he spoke and said"*, as though he spoke twice, not as he spoke at other times, but like a man in defiance, which could not recall any word that he said, but if he could say more, he would say it to anger him. Did I call it *great Babylon?* I may call it *great* Babylon. Did I say that I built it? I will *say* that I built it. Did I add more words for the honor of my majesty? Let it go for the honor of my majesty? In this way, he spoke and said, as though he would be constant in his pride, although he was constant in nothing else.

Is not this great Babylon, that I have built for the house of the kingdom by the might of my power, for the honor of my majesty?

Three things I note in this *saying:*

First, what a glorious opinion Nebuchadnezzar had of his vain buildings seen in these words: *Is not this great Babylon?*

The second is that he phrases himself as the founder of it, as if he had done all without any help in these words: *that I have built for the house of the kingdom by the might of my power.*

The third is that in all of his work he sought nothing but vainglory from these words: *and for the honor of my majesty.*

These three sins of Nebuchadnezzar were revealed in one *brag.* And in these three, we are like him, but the beasts are *not* like him, so he became a beast. First, we do not have as wonderful an opinion of God, or of his word, or of heaven, as we have of our own acts; although we are never able to do half of what Nebuchadnezzar did then, yet this is our manner, to attribute all to ourselves—whether it is riches, honors, health, or knowledge—as if all came by labor, policy, art, or nature. If we cannot draw it to one of these, then we think it is fortune—even though we do not understand what fortune is—for if we counted ourselves obliged to God for them, we would find time to be thankful to him. Lastly, when we overview these matters, our solace and comfort are to think with ourselves, these are the things that make us famous and spoken about and pointed to, and there we end, as though it was enough to be pointed at. *Is not this great Babylon?*

The thing which one loves seems great and precious above all which he does not love, although they are better than it. So do these buildings seem to Nebuchadnezzar. One would think that a fair house was not a matter for a king to be proud of. Stone walls are not so precious that he should repose his entire honor on limestone and mortar. But this is a just thing with God that vain men should have vain prosperity, vain comfort, and vainglory, that they may deceive them when they trust it. Therefore, as the faithful soul looks on the word, or up to heaven, and says to itself: *Is this not my joy, my inheritance?* So the carnal man, when he looks on his buildings, or his money, says to himself: *Is this not my joy, my life?* And while he pores and gapes to long upon it, little by little the love of it grows more and more in his heart, until he thinks of nothing else. This was the first dotage of Nebuchadnezzar.

The second was "*that I have built for the house of the kingdom by the might of my power.*" What a shroud this was to say—that *he* built Babylon—when all history records that it was built by Semiramis before Nebuchadnezzar ever was born. Therefore, does he boast of that which another did? The answer is easy; but why do others now? We see that every man labors to obscure the same of others, that they may shine alone and bear the names, especially in buildings. If they only add or alter anything in their school, or hospitals, or colleges, they look to be counted as founders of them.

And so, the first founders of many ancient places are forgotten; so it is like what Nebuchadnezzar did, to add or alter something in this city, and therefore, he took all to himself. But if Semiramis, or any other had not built it, and only Nebuchadnezzar had been the founder (as he would have you believe), yet this was still a proud and arrogant speech to say—*that I have built*—for it was not he that could build Babylon any more than Nimrod could finish Babylon, but only unless *the Lord build the house, the builders build in vain*, (Psalm 127:1).

Therefore, when he says, *"by the might of my power,"* he should have said, *"by the might of God's power."*

But by this you may plainly discern how hard and difficult it is for him to hit on a right word, or a good work, which does not have a good thought to bring it forth. Therefore, make the root sweet, or the fruit will be sour; counterfeit as cunningly as he can, (Matt. 12:33).

Lastly, where he puts in *"for honor of my majesty,"* he shows that he was of Absalom's honor. Though Absalom had deserved shame, yet he would have fame because he has no children to keep his name in remembrance; therefore, he erected a pillar, which he called Absalom's place. Just as the stately houses in England bear the names of the Lord's that own them, for the same vanity, (2 Sam. 18:17-18).

Here Absalom thought to be buried, as Nebuchadnezzar thought to dwell in his palace, but he was cast into a pit, as Nebuchadnezzar was turned into the wilderness. So Sheba made his sepulcher in one country and was buried in another. For, why should pride have the reward of humility? Solomon says, "...and before honor is humility," (Prov. 18:12). That is, honor is the reward of humility, and yet Nebuchadnezzar would be honored for his pride. What has he done, or Sheba, or Absalom, that they should erect such monuments, to be praised after death which were not worthy to be praised in their life? Before the building of Babylon, he had done nothing worth speaking because he lived like a beast; therefore, God punished him like a beast, (Isa. 22:16-18).

And he deserves now to be spoken of in all ages, for heaping stones together? In this way, we see that a small matter makes great men proud, and they want to be praised for everything they do.

But look how God thwarts them; for that which they look to make their greatest glory, they shame themselves the most of all. And that which they practice to exalt them, disgraces and overthrows them, giving them hatred of such, which otherwise would not meddle with them. Sin deceives them, like the blind Amorites, that they take an opposite way to their desires, as we see in Genesis 11:4; they which built Babylon said that they would build it to make themselves a name, but they received themselves shame; for they could not finish that which they had begun because they were confounded in such a way that they did not know what they were doing. Suddenly, they did not understand a word that one another spoke. So when Nebuchadnezzar came to himself again, he shows that when he sought his own honor and glory, honor and glory both departed from him, and he was made like a beast; but when he sought the honor and glory of God, his honor came again, and he was made a king.

This would pull away many toys from women's backs, if they weighed and considered how God makes them ridiculous by what they wear to make themselves *amiable*. If they thought that the superfluity of apparel, which they put on to please the world, by the secret judgment of God, did not please but displease, they would be as much ashamed of their attire as Eve was of her nakedness. They would wear such garb like a peddler's shop on their backs, only to please. See now how God mocks them, for they are not liked, but disliked, and worse thought of for it than if they go in simple attire and seek no praise at all. They think, *"Am I not splendid?"* Others think, *"Is she not proud?"* They think, *"Am I not sweet?"* Others think, *"Is she not light?"* Yet, they dream that everyone praises them, as Nebuchadnezzar thought that everyone would honor him for his palace.

If their gorgeous buildings and magnificent show condemn them before men, how will it condemn them before God? Therefore, when Nebuchadnezzar says, *"for the honor of his majesty,"* he should have said for the honor of God's majesty, and then this would have been recorded for his honor indeed, and his house would have been the house of God, for as we should speak, study, and labor to God's glory, so we should build also to God's glory that our houses may be like temples as Obadiah's was. But few seek glory that way; they would rather put down than build up. So, you have heard what Nebuchadnezzar spoke, as though God would destroy the thoughts and pride of such builders. These are the thoughts and meditations of princes and nobles, when they behold their buildings, open their coffers, and look upon their train swinging after them; they think as Nebuchadnezzar thought, *Is this* not great Babylon? Is not this glory great? Are not these the treasures that shall make my children rich? Is not this the train that makes me reverenced in the streets? Is not this the house that shall keep my name and cause me to be remembered and make them that are children now to speak of me hereafter? When they shall go by and look up and see these antiques and knick-knacks over their heads, they will say: *Oh, he that built this was a great man; he did bear a great sway in court and country while he lived, although this king is now dead and buried, yet his pride escaped and came to us.* Nebuchadnezzar has children yet alive, which built as high as he, dress as splendid as he, and are as proud and insolent as he; although they are not kings, nor dukes, nor knights, nor yet good squires. Look upon their palaces, and then consider with yourself and think whether they are of Nebuchadnezzar's brood. *Is not this great Babylon?* And is not Nebuchadnezzar lord of it? Oh, if they might still live to walk in their galleries, they would never desire any other heaven.

But Nebuchadnezzar has showed the way before them, and they must all dance after him, though they were as mighty—even mightier—than he, death will not take his kingdom for a ransom. Now what is Babylon and what is Nebuchadnezzar the king of? Now Babylon is destroyed, and the king which built it is laid in dust. Had it not been better to have built a house in heaven, which might have received him when he was dead? The name of these palaces may well be Babylon—that is, confusion—because they prophesy confusion to them which build the palaces; for their foundation is pride; their walls are extortion; their roof is ambition, and all the stuff within them is usury, bribery, and cruelty. Now if this is the best which Nebuchadnezzar has to want, what is the worst which he may be ashamed of? When I see how earnest he was about his dream, and how loose he sat after in his palace, I think I see the image of the world in one man. How lively does

Nebuchadnezzar resemble the dreamers of our time? He had such inquiry, such diligence to know God's will, that a man would have sworn, if the king met with a prophet from heaven who could tell him the truth and instruct him from God about his dream which warned him to amend his life, then he would reclaim himself, reform his realm, and become such a king as was never in this land before. But behold, no sooner resolved of his dream, but he was ready to be warned again, and was not so attentive to the prophets as he was to his dream, though he care for neither, for when he understood that his dream went about to change the course of his life, he went away like Naaman who cared no more for his dream, (2 Kings 5:11). Before the dream came, all would have said that such a dream would have humbled his heart for ever. Before the prophet came, all would have said that such a prophet would have converted him with a word, but Nebuchadnezzar is Nebuchadnezzar, and if any other dream came more fearful than this, yet Nebuchadnezzar will be Nebuchadnezzar, and love his palace *better* than paradise. So we think if God would send a famine on this land that would make us fear him, but God has sent a famine, and yet we do not fear him. If God would send an earthquake on this land that would make us fear him, but God has sent an earthquake on this land, and yet, we do not fear him. If God would send a pestilence on this land, that would make us fear him, but God has sent a pestilence, and yet, we do not fear him. If God would send war upon this land, that would make us fear him, but God has sent war, and yet, we do not fear him. Therefore, what will make us fear him? There are many that dream on religion, as Nebuchadnezzar dreamed on his dream. But he desired only to know what it meant; so do they only desire to know. The young man says to Christ: "Good Master, what shall I do that I may inherit eternal life?" (Mark 10:17). He was pleased to *know* the way to heaven, but when Christ *showed* him the way, he would not *take* it. So they that go from preacher to preacher, as Nebuchadnezzar sent from one wise man to another, to be resolved in points of religion, have such attention and heat, as though they would run beyond the teachers, that a man would think they would do anything, as the Jews seemed to Moses and the young man unto Christ, (Deut. 5:27; Exod. 19:3, 20:19). But when they have heard what they can, they do like Nebuchadnezzar, as they did before. Now they say it was but a dream because the meaning does not answer to his will. So King Ahab inquired of the prophet to see what he would say, (1 Kings 22:15-18), but it appears that the king never meant to follow him, unless he would answer as the king would have him.

When it comes to the act, which is every man's trial, then you shall see who are like Nebuchadnezzar, who only want to know, and who are like Zaccheus, who practice what they know, (Luke 19:8). For as the truth is revealed, so it must be witnessed; otherwise, the fall of Nebuchadnezzar shows what will fall upon it because he would not do as the dream warned him and as the prophet counseled him; therefore, God forsook him, and his kingdom departed from him, and he was thrust out of his palace and turned like an ox into the wilderness, where he lived in all points like a beast until the time of seven years were ended.

A warning to all to take heed of the world, for it is the gentle warning; the next is rougher and the third and fourth are harder than the previous one. Just like the nine plagues of Egypt which exceeded one another, (Exod. 7-10). Who can give weight to the wrath of God, or the grievousness of sin? Some would think that Nebuchadnezzar might have spoken all this, without such offense; for he did say that it was a fair house, and that he built it and erected it for his honor. Many *under princes* delight in worse vanities than building, and speak of more vanities in a week. Therefore, when you see how it displeases God to want of these earthly things, or to impute anything to ourselves, think what will be the doom of greater sins. If Nebuchadnezzar became like a beast and lodged in the wilderness for his pride, they which bear pride, covetousness, lust, wrath, malice, and all legions of sins in one breast, will lodge in hell and become like devils because they are like beasts already. Therefore, let this be instead of Daniel's warning. If God did take such account of Nebuchadnezzar for his dream—what he had profited by it—what account will he take of us— what profit we have made of Nebuchadnezzar's fall and punishment.

In this way, you have heard what the voice spoke from earth. Now you should hear what the voice spoke from heaven, but the time will not permit; therefore, here I end and we will look at this in the next section.

PART 2: THE FALL OF KING NEBUCHADNEZZAR

"While the word was in the king's mouth, there fell a voice from heaven, saying, O king Nebuchadnezzar, to thee it is spoken; The kingdom is departed from thee. And they shall drive thee from men, and thy dwelling shall be with beasts of the field: they shall make thee to eat grass as oxen, and seven times shall pass over thee, until thou know that the most High ruleth in the kingdom of men, and giveth it to whomsoever he will. The same hour was the thing fulfilled upon Nebuchadnezzar: and he was driven from men, and did eat grass as oxen, and his body was wet with the dew of heaven, till his hairs were grown like eagles' feathers, and his nails like birds' claws," (Dan. 4:31-33).

From verse 29 to the end of Daniel 4, the pride, fall, and restitution of Nebuchadnezzar is laid down.

The first two verses are like a banner of his pride, which showed him in his ruffling—as it were—in the air before he knew God or himself. The next three verses are the discovery of his shame, which shows him in his misery—as it were—groveling on the ground after God had cooled his courage. The last four verses are the celebration of his recovery, which showed him in holiness—as it were—raptured into heaven and singing with the saints for joy that God had brought him to his senses, though it was through shame, trouble, and loss of all that he had for seven years. We have already heard in the first section about his *pride*. Yet, we are friends to vices, as we are to men, as long as they prosper and flourish, but when they decay and fall, then we shrink away and are ashamed of them. So it may be, if you could see pride take a fall—though you love her so well—yet, you would forsake her, like a bankruptcy, when you see that she can no longer please you. Therefore, you will see Nebuchadnezzar on his feet again. Before you saw him on his knees, you saw what a king he was in his galleries; but after, you find his servants in his palace, his subjects on his throne, and himself like a beast in the wilderness. May God give you hearts to think a little of this sin, which cost so dear and is common now in every house, as it was then in the king's court.

Daniel says, "At the end of twelve months," (Dan. 4:29); that is, twelve months after God had warned this king by dreams and by Daniel to repent of his sins, he was strutting in his galleries and thought about what sin should be next, as though he had never heard of dreams or prophets.

By this computation of sin—where the months are observed so exactly of how long Nebuchadnezzar rebelled after he was warned—Daniel shows what a reckoning God keeps of our months, weeks, and days, which he gives us to repent, as he did with Nebuchadnezzar. Daniel also shows what an account we shall make of them, as Nebuchadnezzar did, though we count no more of our age than the child does of his youth and have done no more of our task at twenty than we did when we were ten, nor at thirty than when we were twenty, nor at forty than when we were thirty; yet we shall give an account of more hours in the Day of Judgment, and it shall be heavier to the old than to the young and to you which have the word, than to them which want it. And there is a great God between Nebuchadnezzar and us; for he, who challenged Nebuchadnezzar after twelve months since he was warned, may challenge us after twelve years since we were warned, and yet, we do not look for as great a punishment that fell upon Nebuchadnezzar for twelve months. Daniel names twelve months as though he would speak of a great matter and shows how worthy Nebuchadnezzar was to be punished because he might have reformed his life since he was warned. There were twelve months between his dreams and his banishment; but that year, when he had so many warnings and teachings, was as vain as the rest, if not vainer than the years before, because he should have been a mourner like the king of Nineveh when Jonah threatened destruction.

But like a victor of a country returned from battle, to solemnize his triumph Nebuchadnezzar first decked his palace as splendid as himself and then walked his stations in it. When he had set all things before him, which made him forget God, and hoisted himself in pride, like a serpent that would burst unless he discharged some of his poison, Nebuchadnezzar broke out and said: "Is not this great Babylon, that I have built for the house of the kingdom by the might of my power, and for the honor of my majesty?" (Dan. 4:30). Observe first what a glorious opinion this vain king had of his vain buildings. Secondly, observe how he names himself the founder of them, as though he had done all without any help. Thirdly, observe that in all his works he sought nothing but vainglory, as he witnesses against himself, saying: *that I have built for the house of the kingdom by the might of my power, and for the honor of my majesty*, not for the honor of God's majesty, but for the honor of his majesty. So, that which he condemned—as Christ did the beauty of the temple, (Matt. 24:2)—he admired, and nothing seemed so glorious to him, as that which made him shameful to God. Secondly, that city which was built by Semiramis, he arrogated to himself and never joined the chief work-master with him, but said, *that I have built for the house of the kingdom by the might of my power*, when he should have said by the might of God's power. For David says: "Except the Lord build the house, they labor in vain that build it," (Psalm 127:1).

Lastly, that which he should have built for the honor of God—as the man built a chamber for the prophet, (2 Kings 4:10)—Nebuchadnezzar built for his *own* honor. Therefore, when all his pleasures were prepared like a feast, and he came down to the banquet, it happened to him in the same way as to the miserly person in the Gospel, who filled his barns and sang in his heart that his soul should be merry, but all was taken from him that night, and the devils made merry with him in *hell*. So Nebuchadnezzar had feathered his nest and began to crow on his roof: *Is not this great Babylon...*; as if he should say: *Now Nebuchadnezzar make yourself merry.* In that hour his honor was taken from him, for a voice came down from heaven—like the terrible hand which wrote on the wall when Belteshazzar sat at his banquet—and dashed his pride upon a rock. Within an hour all his pomp, pleasures, and treasures suffered shipwreck so that his fall was more admired than his glory and buildings which he himself admired. In this way, all the joy, pleasures, and glory of pride are spoken with one breath and stopped with another.

You have heard what the voice spoke from earth, now you will hear what the voice spoke from heaven. The three verses in Daniel 4:31-33 declare the king's fall by telling when, how, and from whom: *While the word was*—tells the time; *there fell a voice from heaven*—shows the Judge; *saying, O king*—tells the arraignment; *The kingdom is departed*—tells the judgment; *and he was driven from men, and did eat grass as oxen...till his hairs were grown like eagles' feathers*—shows the execution and manner of his punishment. First, we will deal with the time: *While the word was.*

As Daniel observed the time when Nebuchadnezzar *sinned*, so he observes the time when Nebuchadnezzar is *punished*, as if God had lain in wait to catch him in his words and take him when he stumbles—even as he watched Lot's wife and transformed her into a pillar of salt *as soon as* she looked back, (Gen. 19:26). So now, the Lord lays in wait, like a scout, to watch for Nebuchadnezzar's treason and to apprehend him upon it: *O Nebuchadnezzar, you have vaunted these twelve months since I warned you, and I made as though I did not hear, but allowed you to do and speak your pleasure, and do you sill vaunt? Surely, you will no longer escape me; I will not hear a word more against my honor.* So he cut him off while the words were still in his mouth and propounded the words of judgment against him. If you mark the time when the voice spoke from heaven, you may see three wisdoms of God. First, God takes him in his fault so that he might see his fault, as King Jeroboam was afflicted when he "heard the saying of the man of God," (1 Kings 13:4). Secondly, he takes him suddenly because he condemns his warning, as the fire came upon Sodom while they condemned Lot's warning, (Gen. 19:24). Thirdly, God takes him where he is the most pleasant, lustful, and safe in his palace, which was like a castle, as he took Herod when his guard stood by him so that he might see that nothing can guard him from God, but God must guard him from danger, (Acts 12:23). Princes are not safer than their subjects. So though a man sins often and strengthens his sins—as it were—without punishment; yet at the last he is napping while the wickedness is in his hand, as the Jews were when the quails were in their mouths, (Num. 11:33). His day is set when he shall pay for all, whether it is after twelve months, or twelve years; whenever it comes, it will seem too soon. Vengeance stays until the sin is ripe; therefore, watch the time when they are most occupied, for then judgment steps forth like the angel stopped Balaam in his way, (Num. 22:22). Because the punishment is more terrible and grievous when they do not look for it (like Balaam, the worst wish to die the death of the righteous); therefore, God will cross them, even though they always prospered before, yet their end will be a judgment upon all their life and a prophecy of torment for all men to see what becomes of the wicked after death so that they may fear to be like them. As when we see some struck dead while they forswear themselves as the bar of judgment. Some fall down under the table, while they sit swilling at the wine and some are struck dumb in the pulpit, while they preach untruths; even as the Philistines were slain while they feasted, as Herod was shamed while he vaunted, (Acts 12:23), and as Jeroboam was struck when he put forth his hand, (1 Kings 13:4). What does this teach us, but that our sins, as soon as they are done, depart from us and go to the Judge where they accuse us, just as Cain's murder cried out against him as soon as he slew his brother, (Gen. 4:8-10). God says, "I know thy works," (Rev. 3:15). He may say: *I know thy works and thoughts too.* For Judas could not go so closely about his treachery that Christ did know when his thought entered his heart, heard when he conferred also with the scribes, and saw likewise when he took the bribe, though he kept a time to punish him, (Matt. 26:14-16). When he sees a convenient time, then he will execute judgment: "For they shall soon be cut down like the grass, and wither as the green herb," (Psalm 37:2).

Now the time was come when this king should be made an example to all other kings after him, to amend their lives and reform their realm. When the prophet comes from God to them to tell them what they should do—when the dreams and Daniel had done what they could—now God calls forth his judgments and bids them to see what they can do and commands them to chase Nebuchadnezzar until he has (1) lost his kingdom, (2) been driven out of his palace, (3) fled into the wilderness, and (4) become degenerate like a beast, (5) been made the sport of his subjects and servants who gaze and wonder at him like a fool who goes to the stocks or a trespasser who is gazed on in the pillory. So this king was debased when God heard him vaunt of his buildings.

Therefore, let us take heed and be careful after what sort we speak and what words slip from us, lest God takes us in our lies, slanders, or ribaldry as he took Nebuchadnezzar when his tongue walked without a bit. For if he had supposed that God had been so near and that he would have answered him as he did, he would have held his peace and laid his hand on his mouth, rather than pay so dear for a vain word which did him no good when it was spoken.

The second note is of the judge: *there fell a voice from heaven.* The controlling voice came down from heaven. God is most offended with our sin, for Nebuchadnezzar might have spoken more than this before any other man, and no man could control him because he was a king. Kings delight in greater vanities than buildings, yet no man says: *Why do you do this?* For Solomon says, "He that repeateth a matter separateth very friends," (Prov. 17:9). That is, he who tells princes their faults makes them his enemies. Therefore, since John the Baptist died, only God is left to reprove all that sin by authority, yet one is in heaven that has an ear and a tongue that checks the king as boldly as the king checks his subjects. When the voice from earth spoke vainly, the voice from heaven spoke judgment. Here is the king of heaven against the king of earth; the voice of God against the voice of man. A divine wrath warring with human pride; the fire is kindled, woe to the stubble. The Lord of Hosts is in arms against the lord of Babylon and begins to lay hands on him and thrust him out of his throne. First, he rattles him like a thunder: *O king Nebuchadnezzar*, as if he should say: *For though you are a king, you shall see whether another is above you. Now guard your person and defend your honor, for he whom you have despised, threatens to take your kingdom away from you. Go now and walk in your gallery; take one more turn before you are turned out-of-doors and walk with the beasts in the forest.* Now he comes to the arraignment and calls him to the bar: *O king Nebuchadnezzar, to thee it is spoken.* He was never called king with less reverence, nor had such a payment for sin in all his reign. God gives him his title, but he tells him his lot; he calls him king, but without a kingdom—as if he had said, *Late king of Babylon, hold up your hand.* Here a king is arraigned in his own kingdom, and no evidence given against him, but as though he had witnessed against himself (as all sinners do), God condemns him out of his own mouth, and to open his ears, he calls him by his own name, *O king Nebuchadnezzar*, as the prisoner is called when he holds up his hand at the bar. Then he pronounced the judgment: *to thee it is spoken*; or to you who advance yourself like God; or to you who would not take heed by the dream; or to you who did all for your own honor. Now hearken to the judgment: *The kingdom is departed from thee*; you will be driven out of your palace. They who should honor you will expulse you, and you shall reign with the beasts in the desert. You will dwell there seven years; go now and stalk in the woods as you did in your palaces, and when you are among the lions, wolves, and bears, look to Babylon which you have built. How does this speech differ from Nebuchadnezzar's speech? His words were only words, but "he [*God*] spake, and it was done," (Psalm 33:9). For in the same hour that it was spoken, it was done—says Daniel—and whatever the same voice threatens to our sins or to the sinner, shall be done at first or at last. To Nebuchadnezzar it was said, *The kingdom is departed from thee*; to us it is said, Your life will be taken from you. To him it was said, *And they shall drive thee from men*; to us it is said, You will be thrown forth into darkness. To him it was said, *And thy dwelling shall be with beasts of the field*; to us it is said, You shall be like the damned. Shall not the voice spoken to us be remembered with God, as well as the threatening menaced to him?

This voice came from heaven, and therefore, it spoke directly, not like those who glide by the faults of princes and whisper behind their backs, as though they would reprove them if they dare, but for fear that the prince, counselor, judge, or magistrate should take it as he means it and think that he aims at them, which makes them speak in parables, as though they would cast a veil over their reproof and eat their message before they have spoken it. The Holy Spirit teaches us here to reprove so that whoever sins may know that you speak to him. He who speaks from heaven, as this voice did, must speak like John the Baptist among the publicans, harlots, and soldiers, as though he went from one to another and said, *This is spoken to you, this is spoken to you, and this is spoken to you.* For unless we come near the mortal gods and proud Nebuchadnezzars, as near as Elijah came to Ahab when he said, "Art thou he that troubleth Israel?" (1 Kings 18:17), they will post it over and think that you do not speak to them until you speak plainly, as the voice spoke from heaven: *to thee it is spoken.* And then they will reform the matter, or else God shows some judgment on them, as he did here on this great King Nebuchadnezzar. Now the decree goes forth that Nebuchadnezzar will no longer be king, *The kingdom is departed from thee.* This is such a saying, as if Nebuchadnezzar had thought of it before, he would have wept when he vaunted, to think that his honor was going from him, when he thought it was coming to him; yet, his kingdom was not departed from him, and yet, God says, *The kingdom is departed from thee*, because his decree was past, which should surely come to pass, as if it were past already. Therefore, we do not care as long as the prophet says that we *will* die, or we *will* suffer, or we *will* answer, but if he leaves off the "*will*" and "*now*," as God said to Abimelech: "Behold, thou art but a dead man," (Gen. 20:3). He did not say you will die, but you are dead. This roused him more, than if he had threatened him a hundred deaths because he thought that he should die presently. So the Holy Spirit is forced, as it were, to exceed and speak more than we think he should speak because of the hardness of our hearts, which hear like stones and move like snails. If we have but a week to repent, we will defer it to the last day so that we may sin all the rest.

Therefore, it was proper to say, *The kingdom is departed from thee.* Seeing that his judgment should not cease, he should not cease his repentance. If this voice had said that Nebuchadnezzar's Babylon shall sink, as Nimrod's Babylon did, it seems he would have thought his honor buried, but when he was stripped, not only of his palace, but also of his kingdom, what heavy news was this to him, which thought himself equal with God, and now may not be a king. But when he was thrust among beasts to eat grass with oxen, what a downfall this was to be brought under all his subjects, which spoke even now as though there were none but he, and now his servant's servant would not be like to him? So the King of Kings will be honored of kings, as they are of their subjects, or else he will tread on their crowns, and they will hear the same at last, *The kingdom is departed from thee.* Now follows the execution of this judgment, for Daniel says: *The same hour was the thing fulfilled.* So he shows the order of it, as a prisoner is brought to the bar and led to the gallows, so this king was drawn from his throne and turned into the wilderness, where he abode among wild beasts *till his hairs were grown like eagles' feathers, and his nails like birds' claws.*

When God began, he made haste—even though it was long before he spoke—but when he spoke, he did it and affected in an hour all that the dream and the prophet had foretold. Then it was fulfilled: "A man's pride shall bring him low," (Prov. 29:23). Even in that hour that Nebuchadnezzar advanced himself more than before, in the same hour he was brought under all his subjects, servants, and pages, so he who sets up can pull down; he who gave can take; he who made can destroy.

Therefore, let no man vaunt though he were a king of his house, land, farm, or children, but know that he should have nothing, if God did not regard him more than another. And think when you read this story, whether you are not as proud of your wealth as Nebuchadnezzar was of his palace. Whether you are not as proud of your children as Nebuchadnezzar was of his kingdom. Whether you are not as proud of your parentage as Nebuchadnezzar was of his honor. Whether you are not as proud of your learning as Nebuchadnezzar was of his train. If you are not as proud, then God does not say, *O king Nebuchadnezzar, to thee it is spoken* (or: *Oh subject, to you it is spoken, these blessings will be taken away from you*). For, has God taken no man's kingdom from him but Nebuchadnezzar's? Has he taken no man's office from him but Judas'? Has he taken no man's riches from him but Job's? How did Antiochus, Julian, Herod, Saul, Athaliah, Jezebel, and Richard III go from their thrones, as if God had pulled them out by their ears? He had no respect to their persons, but used them like beasts as he did Nebuchadnezzar and fulfilled his threatening. The candle of the wicked will be put out. Therefore, as Christ says to them who turn back to *remember Lot's wife.* So I say to them who bear high minds, proud looks, and stout words remember King Nebuchadnezzar, how God resisted the proud. Now if any man longs to be resolved, how this king was changed to a beast, he must not imagine any strange metamorphosis, or popish transubstantiation, as though his shape were altered, or his manhood removed, or that he put on horns and hoofs, as the poets said of Acteon; for the voice does not say that he should become a beast, but that he should *dwell* with the beasts. Daniel does not say that his head, arm, or legs were transformed, but that the hair of his head and the nails of his fingers grew like eagle's feathers and like bird's claws, as every man's hair and nails will do if he does not pare them. Lastly, Nebuchadnezzar does not say that his shape was restored to him, but that his understanding was restored to him. All which declare that he was not changed in body, but in mind; not in shape, but in quality. A savage mind came on him, like that which drove Cain from the company of men, (Gen. 4:12), and he became like a satyr or wild man, which differs from a beast only in shape. Though he was not turned into a beast, yet this was a strange alteration, to be so changed in an hour that his nobles abhorred him, his subjects despised him, his servants forsook him, and none would company with him, but the beasts. Consider this all that advance themselves against God and despise his word, as Nebuchadnezzar did. Take warning by a king, who even now walked in his galleries, and his nobles served him in his palace with all dishes that the air, sea, or land could afford. Now he is turned to grass and feeds like an ox with the beasts in the wilderness. This was to show that God makes no more account of the wicked than of beasts; and therefore, the Holy Spirit calls them often by the name of beasts, showing how sin and pleasure make men like beasts when they have abused their wits often and persuaded their reason, at last God takes their understanding from them, and they become like beasts, loathsome to themselves and others. Many such beasts we have still like Nebuchadnezzar, who were fitter to live in the desert among lions, where they might not annoy others, than in towns among men, where they infect more than the plague. So, if you have not considered the *beastliness of sin*, look on Nebuchadnezzar *like a beast*. If you would see the guilt of it, look upon wandering Cain, (Gen. 4:12). If you would see the frenzy of it, look on frantic Saul, (1 Sam. 16:14). If you would see the fear of it, look upon trembling Belshazzar, (Dan. 5:6). If you would see the shame of it, look upon Haman hanging upon his own gallows, (Esther 7:10). If you would see the end of it, look upon the pains of *frying in hell*, (Luke 16:23). These are pictures of sin, which God has set for a terror before us, like the pillar of salt, (Gen. 19:26), or Achan's sepulcher, (Josh. 7:26), to speak to us. Take heed by those, for God says, when I have warned you, as I warned them, I will punish you, as I punished them.

This is the epitaph, as it were, which God engraved on Nebuchadnezzar's sepulcher:

Be thou an example to kings and rulers, for

all the children of price to beware how they set

themselves against him who advanced them.

So, he which sets up, can pull down. Did I not send you dreams to warn you? Did I not send a prophet to warn you? If either of them would have served, you might have ruled still, walked in your galleries, feasted in your palace, judged on your throne, and died a king. But now your kingdom is departed from you, who would be like Nebuchadnezzar, now that the king is like a beast? If this heathen was thus challenged for his warning, when he had heard only one prophet, we may tremble to think that we will answer for our warning, which have been threatened as often as the Israelites, and yet provoke the Lord while he serves us, like those which curse the sun while it hits on them.

So, you have seen the fall of pride. Even though he said, "Is not this great Babylon?" (Dan. 4:30). Now, he may say, *Is not this unhappy Babylon?* Even though he said, "...that I have built for the house of the kingdom," (Dan. 4:30). And now, he may say, *That I have built by the vanity of my pride*. Even though he said: "by the might of my power," (Dan. 4:30). Now, may he say: *For the ruin of my kingdom*; yet, after this he rose again, came to himself, received his kingdom, and honored him which punished him so. But the time will prevent me to speak of his restitution now. Therefore, I end here, next to treat the restitution of the king.

PART 3: THE RESTITUTION OF KING NEBUCHADNEZZAR

"While the word was in the king's mouth, there fell a voice from heaven, saying, O king Nebuchadnezzar, to thee it is spoken; The kingdom is departed from thee. And they shall drive thee from men, and thy dwelling shall be with beasts of the field: they shall make thee to eat grass as oxen, and seven times shall pass over thee, until thou know that the most High ruleth in the kingdom of men, and giveth it to whomsoever he will. The same hour was the thing fulfilled upon Nebuchadnezzar: and he was driven from men, and did eat grass as oxen, and his body was wet with the dew of heaven, till his hairs were grown like eagles' feathers, and his nails like birds' claws. And at the end of the days I Nebuchadnezzar lifted up mine eyes unto heaven, and mine understanding returned unto me, and I blessed the most High, and I praised and honored him that liveth for ever, whose dominion is an everlasting dominion, and his kingdom is from generation to generation," (Dan. 4:31-34).

Now we come to Nebuchadnezzar's restitution. First Nebuchadnezzar was humbled, as God humbles his enemies; now he is humbled, as God humbles his children. Although he has more honor than he had before, yet he is not proud of it— as he was—but cries with the prophet: "Not unto us, O Lord, not unto us, but unto thy name give glory," (Psalm 115:1). So he who said, not only in heart, but with his mouth too: "There is no God," (Psalm 14:1); now with heart and mouth, honor none but God. Daniel declared Nebuchadnezzar's pride and fall, but when it came to restitution, God makes Nebuchadnezzar speak with him and give thanks to him, like a witness brought in to testify the truth of this wonderful narrative.

When the prophet showed how this king vaunted, and how he was debased for it after he had spoken, he calls in—as it were—the king to witness his report, and he declared how he was raised again, like a man, who having received the grace of a prince or great personage, is brought in before him, to give thanks for his favor received, and then he is dismissed.

In these verses, two things show themselves at first view, Nebuchadnezzar's restitution and thankfulness. In his restitution he shows the time when he was restored in these words: *And at the end of the days.* Then he shows the manner how he was restored in these words, "I Nebuchadnezzar lifted up mine eyes unto heaven, and mine understanding returned unto me...at the same time my reason returned unto me, and for the glory of my kingdom, mine honor and brightness returned unto me; and my counselors and my lords sought unto me; and I was established in my kingdom, and excellent majesty was added unto me," (Dan. 4:34, 36). In his thankfulness he first extolled God's power in setting him up, pulling him down, and raising him again.

Then he commended God's truth and justice, which deserve to be praised for his judgment as much as his mercies, as if he rejoiced that God made him like a beast that he may die like a man *at the end of the days.* The time of his pride was noted when he walked in his palace, to show how his pride grew out of buildings, wealth, apparel, and such roots. The time of his fall was noted when the words were in his mouth, to show that he was punished for his pride and arrogance so that he might know where to begin his conversion and abate his pride. When he had taken away the cause, then God would take away the punishment. So likewise, he noted the time of his restitution, *at the end of the days.* That is, after seven years were expired, to show how long the sickness of pride is in curing and to show how everything was fulfilled—as it was prophesied—even to the point of time. For it was told to him by Daniel that he should be like a beast seven years. Therefore, Nebuchadnezzar is prompt to confess the truth and says—like the prophet said—*at the end of the days.* That is, at the end of seven years, he was restored again to his understanding and honor, as Daniel foretold.

Yet another note is set upon this, lest we should think that God regarded only the season and that seven years of punishment is enough for such a sinner. Nebuchadnezzar says that his understanding and honor were not only restored at the end of seven years, but that they were also restored to him when he began to lift up his eye to heaven to show that his blessing came from above; the God who humbled him had also restored him again. Nebuchadnezzar would say to all that are cast down with sickness, poverty, infamy, or any trouble in body or mind, *He who has humbled you will raise you as he has done to me, but you must first look up to heaven and lift up your heart to him, and then your understanding, comfort, peace, health, wealth, liberty, and good name will return you again like Job's sheep, camels, and oxen which came in a greater number than he had before,* (Job 42). As all the blessings of God returned to Nebuchadnezzar when he looked *up* to heaven, they shall come back like a river on you when your eyes go beyond these vanities and look upon him who looked upon you, or else seven years shall pass over you, and you shall never be better, but worse and worse like Saul, who was vexed more and more until he had killed himself, (1 Sam. 31:4). Therefore, as the Jews looked upon the brazen serpent, which was a figure of Jesus Christ, and were healed, (Num. 21:8); so all who desire to recover what they have lost or to obtain what they want, Nebuchadnezzar teaches them here to lift up their eyes to heaven where, says Christ, every blessing of man comes from.

And at the end of the days I Nebuchadnezzar lifted up mine eyes unto heaven. Like a man who is wakened out of a long trance, now he began to stir and lift up his eyes. When the heart is lifted up, it will lift up the eyes, hands, voice, and all to heaven. He, who never looked up to heaven as long as his comfort was on the earth, has now changed his mind, along with his looks, gestures, and speeches. God shows a visible difference between the spiritual and the carnal in their gate, looks, and gestures, just like the difference between a child and an old man. The spiritual minds are heavenly minds, and they look up because their joy is above. The carnal minds are earthly minds, and they look down like beasts because their treasure is beneath. As the serpent grovels upon the ground, so the serpents feed and have no countenance of grace, (Gen. 3:14). Therefore, by lifting up his eyes to heaven, it is signified that the time had come which the Lord had set down that Nebuchadnezzar should be like a beast until he had well-learned that lesson: that the most High bears rule over the kingdoms of men and gives it to whoever he will.

Therefore, Nebuchadnezzar shows that he had learned this lesson because he looked up to heaven not to behold the sun, moon, or stars like astronomers, but to think how he had set himself against heaven, where all his honor had come from. In godly shame and holy anger towards himself, he turned his face from earth to heaven to magnify God who had humbled, condemned, and advanced him so.

Now he talked no more of his palace, power, or majesty, even though they were greater than before, but he looked above his own palace, up to another palace, where the terrible voice came from saying, *The kingdom is departed from thee*, which expressed his contrite heart and wounded spirit. How many passions battled within, as if he should chide himself and say, *Oh, unthankful man, my power descended from above, but I always looked upon the earth; mine honor came down upon from heaven, and I never lifted up my eyes before. Lift up my eyes, heart, voice, and hands. How long will you gaze upon earth like a beast?* So he lifted up his eyes to heaven. After he had lifted up his eyes, he began to pray and gave praise and thanks to God, which showed that he not only lifted up his eye, but also his heart. For unless we can say with David, "Unto thee, O Lord, do I lift up my soul," (Psalm 25:1), it is in vain to lift up hands, eyes, or voices, as the hypocrites do because he that is a spirit requires the spirit, (John 4:24). "And Mary said, My soul doth magnify the Lord," (Luke 1:46). As for the infidels and idolaters, they have no heart service, but their religion is like an occupation which is done with the body. When we read of the sacrifice or prayers of idolaters, we do not find that they lift up their hearts to the idols, but their hands, eyes, or voices just like the Baalites roared to Baal, (1 Kings 18:28), the mariners cried to their sea gods, (Jonah 1:5), and the Ephesians shouted to Diana, (Acts 19:28). But the lifting up of the heart in service to God is always appropriate because God says: "My son, give me thine heart, and let thine eyes observe my ways," (Prov. 23:26). Therefore, Nebuchadnezzar lifted up his heart to God showing that he had learned the lesson God gave him seven years to study, that the Most High bears rule *over* the kingdoms of men. Now God thought that the time was long enough, and just as he reformed the ground after the Flood with fruits, herbs, and flowers again, so he reformed Nebuchadnezzar with understanding, beauty, and honor again; as if he had repented himself and said, *I will drown the earth no more*, (Gen. 8:21); *I will change Nebuchadnezzar no more. He now knows that there is a King above him; he shall be a king again. He now seeks my honor; I will give him honor. He now magnifies me that debased him, so I will return to exalt him.* So the voice which thundered from heaven—*the kingdom is departed from thee*—sounded again—the kingdom is returned to you. For it was not told him that he should be like a beast until he died, but until he knew that the Most High bears rule over the kingdoms of men. Therefore, when he knew this, nothing could keep him from his kingdom, no more than they could keep him in his kingdom before.

So, the displeasure of God is but an *interim*, until we know something that we should know, and then Nebuchadnezzar shall be a king again (or the sick man shall be whole again or the bond man shall be free again). His mercies are called everlasting because they endure forever, (Psalm 136:1), but his anger is compared to the clouds because it lasts only for a season. Whomever he loves, he loves to the end; but whomever he scourges, he scourges until they repent. Just as Hezekiah was sick until he wept, (2 Kings 20:1-3), so Nebuchadnezzar was banished until he repented. Now the first cure of this king's restitution was his mind: "I Nebuchadnezzar lifted up mine eyes unto heaven, and mine understanding returned unto me...at the same time my reason returned unto me," (Dan. 4:34, 36). He said this to show what inestimable gifts our understanding and reason are, and that we are different from the beasts, for which we cannot be thankful enough. Therefore, he records it twice, as though his heart did flow with gladness, and his tongue could not choose but to speak of it often, as a man thinks and speaks of that which he loves. *Mine understanding returned unto me—* that which was first taken away came first again. As soon as it was gone, he was counted a man no more, but a beast. Just as David said: "Be ye not as the horse, or as the mule, which have no understanding,"

(Psalm 32:9), he accounts them which are void of understanding no better than a horse or mule.

Therefore, they who have left their understanding at the taverns (as many here have done sometime), and they who do not yet understand the Book of God are horse and mule, though they bear the visors of men. After he said, "At the same time my reason returned unto me," he also annexes, "mine honor and brightness returned unto me," (Dan. 4:36), and so he grew to be a king again. As he was accustomed to put on one robe after another when he was king, so when God would make him king again, he put on him the robe of understanding first, as it were, the foundation of a king (like the princely spirit which came upon Saul, (1 Sam. 10:9)), and when he had a princely heart, then God gave him a princely power and proclaimed like a voice from heaven, *Nebuchadnezzar, king of Babylon.* He rose again gloriously like the sun with a triumph of his restitution and welcomed his subjects like the shout that went before King Solomon: "God save king

Solomon," (1 Kings 1:39). It does not appear that his nobles and subjects were converted like himself, to receive him to his kingdom again because he repented, or because it was God's will, but because it was God's will they could not resist it. They fulfilled his ordinance, as the wicked do those things which are foretold that they should do, and never think how they are moved to it, nor which way it comes to pass, no more than the raven knew who had been sent to feed Elijah, (1 Kings 17:4); she did as God commanded her, so they do as God enforces them, but they know not how God enforces them.

One would think that when Nebuchadnezzar was a king, God could never have made him like a beast, and when he was like a beast, one would think that God could never have made him like a king; for who would allow a beast to rule over them unless they were beast themselves. We will not have this man to rule over us, say the Jews (such stomachs are in men that they will hardly abide any man to rule over them). Therefore, it is strange that these men should receive one that had been seven years a beast; it is even as if one should lie seven years in the grave and after come again to challenge his goods, lands, house, and money from them that have taken possession and count it their own. He should have a cold suit of it I think, unless it was some few that loved him in his life, he might go again to his grave for a house to dwell in. So nobody looked now for Nebuchadnezzar to come out of the wilderness; he was the unlikeliest man in the world to be king after such a change. But see what God can do, though all are against it, he who made a king like a beast, raised a king of a beast. Nebuchadnezzar said, *my reason returned unto me*, and more than that, *mine honor and brightness returned unto me*, and more than that, *I was established in my kingdom*, and more than that, *excellent majesty was added unto me*, when he was so proud of it. As God turned his heart, so he turned the heart of his nobles and people that they received him for their king again and reverenced him for all his former disgrace, for which they condemned him before as a beast, here a wise man may stand and wonder, like Elisha when his master was taken to heaven, (2 Kings 2:11-12). Just as a snuff was taken from the ground, set up again the candlestick, and shined brighter than it did before, so the king was raised from the dust and set on the throne. Even now no man cared for him, and now no man dared to displease him; this fulfilled what Solomon said, "When a man's ways please the Lord, he maketh even his enemies to be at peace with him," (Prov. 16:7). So when Nebuchadnezzar pleased the Lord, God gave him grace with men, and his glory was augmented, "I was established in my kingdom, and excellent majesty was added unto me," (Daniel 4:36). He received not only his kingdom, power, and honor again, but he also received usury of them for his seven years of banishment. They have been put out seven years to bank for him, to receive more when he came again. So when he sought his own honor, honor departed from him, his palace could not hold it, his treasures could not redeem it, his guard could not stay it, but pride chased it away while he followed after it. But when he sought God's honor and cared not for his own, then his honor was increased, for God says: "...for them that honor me I will honor," (1 Sam. 2:30). What encouragement is this for all kings like Nebuchadnezzar to seek the honor of God, seeing he has linked his honor with their honor, that they cannot seek God's honor without finding their own honor. Therefore, what would Nebuchadnezzar say to our kings like him who think that it is against their honor to seek Christ's honor, and that if Christ's kingdom is up, their kingdom should go down—like Herod, who thought he could not be king if Christ should reign, and the Pharisees, who thought they should be despised if Christ was regarded. If Nebuchadnezzar's honor came to him because of the honor he gave to God, how long will the honor of those last who eat and drink, give and take, bid and forbid, set up and pull down, favor and wrong, and do all they do to honor themselves (just like Nebuchadnezzar built Babylon until that voice thundered from heaven: *The kingdom is departed from thee*; your office is departed from you; your life is departed from you)? Some have exalted themselves like Nebuchadnezzar and are not fallen yet. Some mounted up and are fallen already. Some are fallen lower and lower like Babylon, but they are not yet at the ground. They have ruled like beasts, longer than he, and yet do not look up to heaven that they might be changed. So, Nebuchadnezzar is welcomed to the throne again. Now he has *received grace*, let us examine his thankfulness. If you mark everything in his order, you shall see a marvelous consequence observed both in his fall and restitution. When he looked on his palace, he waxed proud; when he waxed proud, God threatened him; when he was threatened, God banished him; when he was banished, then he lifted up his eyes to heaven; when his understanding came to him, then he gave thanks to God, showing us the use of our understanding of why God has given reason to man: *videlicet*, to serve him and praise him on earth. Nebuchadnezzar worshipped God and soon came to his understanding. As we come to years of discretion and begin to understand, we should begin a new life and serve him whom all creatures do serve with us, or else our understanding is in vain, and we are like beasts still. For by this Nebuchadnezzar shows that he had understanding and was like a man because he gave praise to God and was moved in his heart to worship God who made him according to David's definition of understanding, "a good understanding have all they that do his commandments," (Psalm 111:10). They who observe the commandments have a good understanding, not they who speak of the commandments, nor they who write of the commandments, nor they who preach of the commandments, but they who keep the commandments have a good understanding. The rest have a false understanding, a vain understanding, an understanding like the scribes and Pharisees, which was enough to condemn them, but not to save them. Besides, every man should try his wisdom because as soon as understanding comes to him, as it came to

Nebuchadnezzar, it will extort prayer and obedience from him, whether he will or not.

Therefore, our kings like Nebuchadnezzar are still beasts because this is not part of their understanding. But he who can go beyond all in shifts and politics is counted the wisest man in the court or city. Oh, if Nebuchadnezzar had lived in our country, what a monarch he might be; to what honor, wealth, and power might he have risen in a short time, whether he had been a lawyer, courtier, or prelate. I think I see how many fingers would point at him in the streets as they do at apes and say, *He has more wit in his little finger than the rest have in their whole body, but we speak to the belly, which has no ears.*

Now, let us see the parts of this king's confession that we may see how his thankfulness answered to his sin, before he had robbed God of his honor. Now, as though he came to make restitution, he brings praise, thanks, and glory in his mouth. First, he advances God's power and says: *whose dominion is an everlasting dominion;* with these words he confesses that God was above him because Nebuchadnezzar's kingdom was not an everlasting kingdom, but a momentary kingdom, like a spark which rises from the fire and falls to the fire again. Therefore, he shows what a fool he was to vaunt of his kingdom, as though it were like God's kingdom which lasts forever. Secondly, he magnifies the power of God and says that God does what he pleases in heaven and in earth, and nothing can hinder him, nor say to him: *What do you do?* Under which words he confesses again that God was above him because he could not reign as he pleased, but when he thought to live at his pleasure, then he as thrust out-of-doors, and God said to him, *The kingdom is departed from thee.* Therefore, he shows what a fool he was to vaunt his power, as though it had been like God's power, which could not be checked. Thirdly, he commends the justice of God and says that his works were all true and his ways were all judgment. Under which words Nebuchadnezzar confesses again that God was above him. For his ways were all errors and his works were all sins as the end proved. Therefore, he shows what a fool he was to vaunt of his works, as though they had been like God's work, which cannot be blamed. Therefore, he concludes, "Now I Nebuchadnezzar praise and extol and honor the King of heaven," (Daniel 4:37). When he lighted on the right string, mark how he harps upon it and doubles and trebles it, like a bond, which is ratified with many words of like sense; so he ratifies his bond to God with many words of like meaning (praise and extol and honor) as though he would praise and then praise him more. So they, who love from the heart, repent from the bottom, praise and praise, pray and pray, give and give, and serve and serve; that is, when they have served him, they are ready to serve him again.

Here is a looking glass for all the children of pride. First, you who are great men look on Nebuchadnezzar, for God will make his examples of great men because they should be examples to others. Many wicked men died in jury and scarcely a man would see their end, but Herod was stricken before the people so that all might see because he was a wicked king. There were many in Babylon as proud as Nebuchadnezzar, but none but Nebuchadnezzar was made a beast because he was a proud king. So God stomachs sin in those that bear his own person. As princes use to pick out the principal and chief of the rebellion, to make them examples of terror, who were ring leaders in the treason, so God bends his shot against the captains of his enemies. Like the king of Aram, who charged his soldiers that they should fight only against Ahab the king, (2 Chron. 18:30). For as Solomon said, "Smite the scorner, and the simple will beware," (Prov. 19:25); so justice shows on a great man and terrifies many. If we could see only one of the kings like Nebuchadnezzar in our day so disgraced, it would make all the rest better in their office and think when they sit in their majesties, as Queen Esther did, that their power is given them to minister justice and not to do wrong. Paul does not wish more wealth for

King Agrippa, nor more honor, nor more friends, but more *religion*, which is the greatest lack of princes and magistrates. David says that they sit in God's chair and are called *gods*, (Psalm 82:6), but they are not like God, but like mammon, except for their names and their crowns. Perhaps there is a David, or a Solomon, or a Joshua, that is, a few that remembers whose person they bear. The rest are like Herod, and Saul, and Nebuchadnezzar, who do not know from whom their kingdoms come. Nebuchadnezzar built his for their honors; he gathered for his wealth, and they gathered for their wealth. He sought his pleasure, and they seek after their pleasures. He vaunted of his power, and they vaunt of their power. What did Nebuchadnezzar do, that they do not, but repent, which they do not? I cannot wish them beasts to do them good like Nebuchadnezzar because it is a question whether they are worse than beasts already. But if we could drive them out of their palace to live in the wilderness, it would be a good riddance, for there they should do less harm.

In this way you see why Nebuchadnezzar was made like a beast that he may die like a man, for he could never learn from whom his kingdom came, or who gave him his name, unless he had been seven years a prentice to the cross. When he perceived who took his kingdom from him, then he gave his kingdom to him and learned his thankfulness in the wilderness.

When all the blessings were gone which he should have been thankful for, he thought God was nobody, until he became like nobody himself; and then who but God, no power but of him, no honor but from him, his first honor came from God, as well as the last, but then he was like a beast, which does not know his owner—like a babe, who does not know his father or like an image, which does not know its maker. But now he does not know his maker. But now he knows from whom kingdoms come and has learned to say, *your kingdom, as well as my kingdom*. And is like the elders in the Revelation, who cast down their crowns before the Lamb. Such a schoolmaster is affliction, to teach that which prophets and angels cannot teach. For the prophet and his dream told him as much before, yet he could never say, *the Lord has given*, before he saw the Lord had taken. They say a friend is never known before he is lost, so when God fled, Nebuchadnezzar followed, but when God called, Nebuchadnezzar condemned when he has all things, he is unthankful, and when he has nothing, he begins to be thankful. So we must learn God's love out of God's wrath; spell his goodness out of his justice. Therefore, we preach judgment to you, to make you fly to mercy. We denounce the law against you, to make you love the Gospel. We show you hell, to make you seek heaven because we are all like Pharaoh's sorcerers. Though we receive never so much, yet we never say, *the finger of God has done this*, but when he begins to plague us, then we cry, *the finger of God has done this*; therefore, if we will not be invited, it is good to be compelled. To conclude, he who made Nebuchadnezzar a king, when he was like a beast, is he that makes the rich, who were poor; and he who makes them free that were slaves; and he who makes them beloved, that were hated; and he who makes them wise, that were rude; and he who makes them whole, that were sick. They must stay a time—seven days or seven weeks, or seven months, or seven years—as Nebuchadnezzar did, when they are ready for it, it will come suddenly, as the angels came to refresh Christ as soon as he was hungry; yet a little while, yet a little longer, comfort is on foot, and that God who is coming, as the sun which was rising, is risen. For as Nebuchadnezzar said, *mine honor and brightness returned unto me*; so I am sure, many here who have been afflicted may say, *my right was restored to me; my liberty was restored to me, my goods were restored to me; my health was restored to me in less time than Nebuchadnezzar's honor was, and what then? Therefore, I Nebuchadnezzar praise and extol and honor the King.* This is the conclusion of all God's benefits. They who do not praise, extol and honor the King of heaven are *worse* than

Nebuchadnezzar. Therefore, let all those who have said in their heart like Nebuchadnezzar, *Is not this the house which I have built? Is not this the land which I have purchased? Is not this the money which I have gathered? Are not those the children who I have begotten?* Say now with Nebuchadnezzar for all, *I praise and extol and honor the King of heaven, who can take all again as he did from Nebuchadnezzar.*

Thus, you have seen pride and humility, one pulling Nebuchadnezzar out of his throne, the other lifting him to his throne, by which they who stand may take heed lest they fall, and they who are fallen, may learn to rise again.

FINIS.

This work was originally printed by

T.S. and sold by *William Wright.*

LONDON,

1591.

www.ingramcontent.com/pod-product-compliance
Lightning Source LLC
Chambersburg PA
CBHW031004090426
42737CB00008B/676